GOD

48 FAMOUS AND FASCINATING MINDS TALK ABOUT GOD

Compiled by Jennifer Berne
Illustrated by R. O. Blechman

RUNNING PRESS
PHILADELPHIA

Printed in China

Books published by Running Press are available at special discounts for bulk purchases in the United States by corporations, institutions, and other organizations. For more information, please contact the Special Markets Department at Perseus Books, 2300 Chestnut Street, Suite 200, Philadelphia, PA 19103, or call (800) 810-4145, ext. 5000, or e-mail special.markets@perseusbooks.com.

ISBN 978-0-7624-6232-2
Library of Congress Control Number: 201696321

E-book ISBN 978-0-7624-6233-9

9   8   7   6   5   4   3   2   1
Digit on the right indicates the number of this printing

Cover and Interior design by Joshua McDonnell
Edited by Jennifer Kasius
Typography: Bembo

Running Press Book Publishers
2300 Chestnut Street
Philadelphia, PA 19103-4371

Visit us on the web!
www.runningpress.com

Introduction

by Jennifer Berne

God is the most omnipresent, most influential, most enduring entity in all of human civilization—all cultures, all time. God is a subject over which great empires, religions, and nations have been built; wars have been waged; magnificent art, music, literature, and architecture have been created; and lives have been lived. Yet God is invisible, and God's very existence is controversial.

So what could be more fascinating than getting a look at how some of humanity's most creative, most brilliant, most interesting minds experience and express their own personal God?

Thus, this book.

Here you'll encounter God through these 48 fascinating minds:

Frank Lloyd Wright

Rumi

John Lennon

Alan Watts

Albert Einstein

Tycho Brahe

Timothy Leary

Galileo Galilei

Virginia Woolf

Jane Goodall

e.e. cummings

Ralph Waldo Emerson

Thomas Edison

H.L Mencken

Julian Barnes

Aldous Huxley

Charles Baudelaire

Maya Angelou

Helen Keller

Ansel Adams

Leonard Cohen

Rainer Maria Rilke

Elie Wiesel

Anne Frank

Lenny Bruce

Emily Dickinson

Frederick Douglass

George Washington Carver

Malala Yousafzai

Mother Teresa

Annie Dillard

Donald Miller

Pope Francis

Susan B. Anthony

Charles de Montesquieu

Rabbi Mark Sameth

Mahatma Gandhi

Will Durant

Salman Rushdie

Eugene O'Neill

Oscar Wilde

Carl Sandburg

Andy Rooney

John Buchan, Lord Tweedsmuir

Kurt Vonnegut

Friedrich Nietzsche

Henry Miller

Sir Richard Francis Burton

A Note from the Illustrator:

When I was asked to illustrate a book about
God I hesitated. God? I'm not really a believer,
so I may be the wrong artist. But then I thought,
well, art, when it's honest and has something to
say to people, has a spiritual aspect. And what is
religion but spiritual?

So here I am, the 49th person, only with pen
and brush, talking about God.

~ R. O. Blechman

All that we can learn of God
we will learn from the body of
God, which we call nature.

~ Frank Lloyd Wright

I looked for God. I went to a temple and
I didn't find him there. Then I went to a
church and I didn't find him there. Then
I went to a mosque and I didn't find
him there. Then finally I looked in my
heart and there he was.

~ Rumi

I believe in God, but not as one thing, not as an old man in the sky. I believe that what people call God is something in all of us. I believe that what Jesus and Mohammed and Buddha and all the rest said was right. It's just that the translations have gone wrong.

~ John Lennon

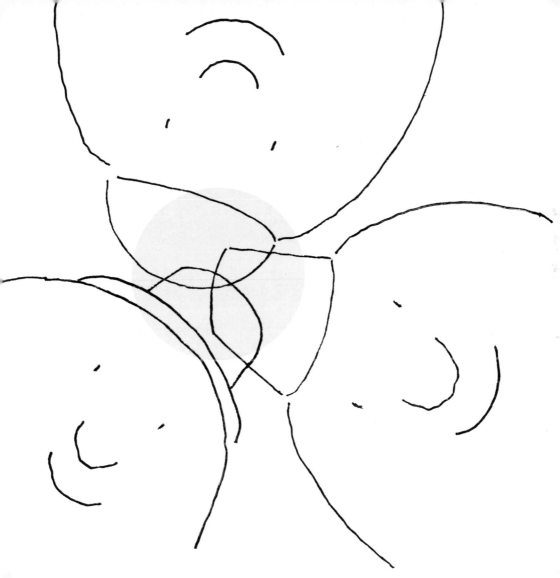

God is what nobody admits to being, and everybody really is. You don't look out there for God, something in the sky, you look inside you.

~ Alan Watts

I believe in Spinoza's God who reveals Himself in the orderly harmony of what exists, not in a God who concerns Himself with the fate and actions of human beings.

~ Albert Einstein

Those who study the stars have God for a teacher.

~ Tycho Brahe

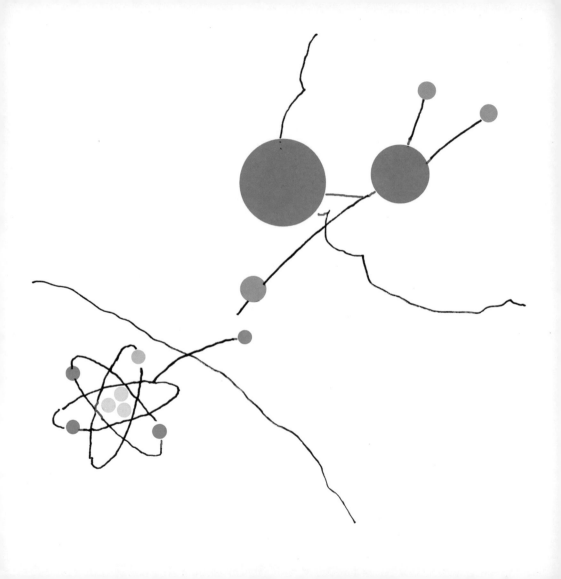

The language of God is not English or Latin;

the language of God is cellular and molecular.

~ Timothy Leary

Mathematics is the language in which God wrote the universe.

~ Galileo Galilei

Nothing is commoner than to assume that of Gods there is only one, and of religions none but the speaker's.

~ Virginia Woolf

I don't think that faith, whatever you're being faithful about, really can be scientifically explained. And I don't want to explain this faith through truth, science. There's so much mystery. There's so much awe.

~ Jane Goodall

i thank You God for most this amazing day,

for the leaping greenly spirits of trees,

and a blue true dream of sky

and for everything which is natural,

which is infinite, which is yes.

~ e. e. cummings

God Himself does not speak prose, but
communicates with us by hints, omens,
inference, and dark resemblances in
objects lying around us.

~Ralph Waldo Emerson

What a wonderfully small idea mankind has of the Almighty. My impression is that he has made unchangeable laws to govern this and billions of other worlds and that he has forgotten even the existence of this little mote of ours ages ago.

~ Thomas Edison

It is impossible to imagine the universe run by a wise, just, and omnipotent God, but it is quite easy to imagine it run by a board of gods.

~ H. L. Mencken

I don't believe in God, but I miss Him. That's what I say when the question is put. I asked my brother, who has taught philosophy at Oxford, Geneva, and the Sorbonne, what he thought of such a statement, without revealing that it was my own. He replied with a single word: "Soppy."

~ Julian Barnes

All gods are homemade, and it is
we who pull their strings, and so,
give them the power to pull ours.

~ **Aldous Huxley**

God is the only being who need not even exist in order to reign.

~ Charles Baudelaire

Whenever I began to question whether God exists, I looked up to the sky and surely there, right there, between the sun and moon, stands my grandmother, singing a long meter hymn, a song somewhere between a moan and a lullaby and I know faith is the evidence of things unseen.

~ Maya Angelou

I do not see a man-made world; I see a God-made world.

~ Helen Keller

Sometimes I arrive just when God's ready to have someone click the shutter.

~ **Ansel Adams**

God is alive. Magic is afoot.

~ Leonard Cohen

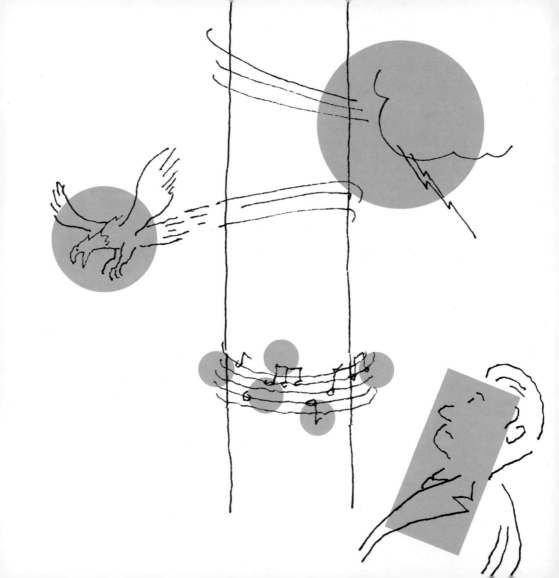

I am circling around God, around the ancient tower,
and I have been circling for a thousand years, and still I
don't know if I am a falcon, or a storm, or a great song.

~ Rainer Maria Rilke

I rarely speak about God.
To God yes. I protest
against Him. I shout
at Him. But to open
a discourse about the
qualities of God, about
the problems that God
imposes, theodicy, no.
And yet He is there, in
silence, in filigree.

~ Elie Wiesel

The best remedy for those who are afraid, lonely, or unhappy is to go outside, somewhere where they can be alone quite with the heavens, nature, and God. Because only then does one feel that all is as it should be and that God wishes to see people happy, amidst the simple beauty of nature.

~ Anne Frank

Every day people are
straying away from the
church and going back
to God.

~ **Lenny Bruce**

We pray to Him, and he answers 'No.' Then we pray to Him to rescind the 'no,' and He don't answer at all, yet 'Seek and ye shall find' is the boon of faith.

~ Emily Dickinson

I prayed for twenty years but received no answer until I prayed with my legs.

~ Frederick Douglass

When I was young, I said to God, god, tell me the mystery of the universe. But God answered, that knowledge is for me alone. So I said, god, tell me the mystery of the peanut. Then god said, well, George, that's more nearly your size.

~ George Washington Carver

Once I had asked God for one or two extra inches in height, but instead he made me as tall as the sky, so high that I could not measure myself . . . By giving me this height to reach people, he has also given me great responsibilities.

~ Malala Yousafzai

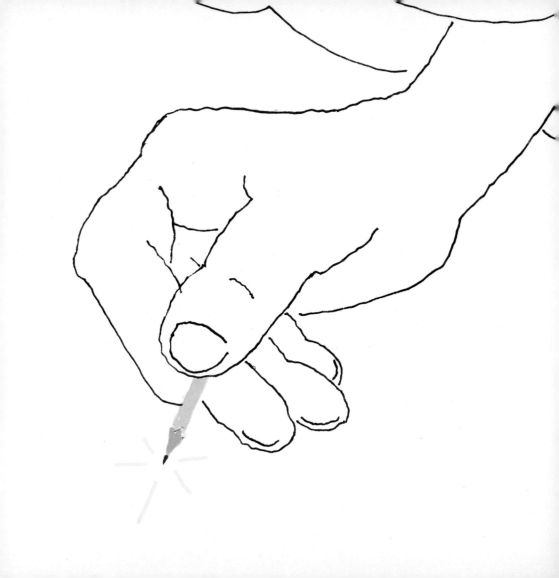

I am nothing but a little pencil in the hand of God. It is He who writes, it is He who thinks, it is He who decides.

~ Mother Teresa

Does anyone have the foggiest idea what
sort of power we so blithely invoke? . . .
It's madness to wear ladies' straw hats
and velvet hats to church; we should be
wearing crash helmets. Ushers should issue
life preservers and signal flares; they should
lash us to our pews. For the sleeping god
may wake someday and take offense, or the
waking god may draw us out to where we
can never return.

~ Annie Dillard

I can no more understand the totality of God than the pancake
I made for breakfast understands the complexity of me.

~ Donald Miller

If one has the answers to all the questions—that is proof that God is not with him. It means that he is a false prophet using religion for himself. The great leaders of the people of God, like Moses, have always left room for doubt. You must leave room for the Lord, not for our certainties; we must be humble.

~ Pope Francis

I distrust those people who know so well what God wants them to do, because I notice it always seems to coincide with their own desires.

~ Susan B. Anthony

There is a very good saying that if triangles invented a god, they would make him three-sided.

~ **Charles de Montesquieu**

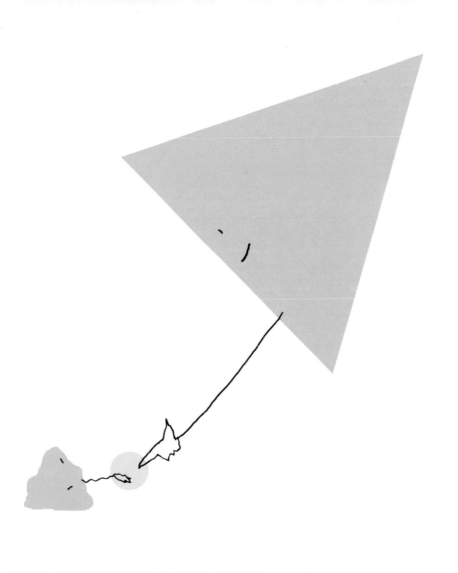

Counter to everything we grew up believing, the God of Israel—the God of the three monotheistic, Abrahamic religions to which fully half the people on the planet today belong—was understood by its earliest worshipers to be a dual-gendered deity.

~ Rabbi Mark Sameth

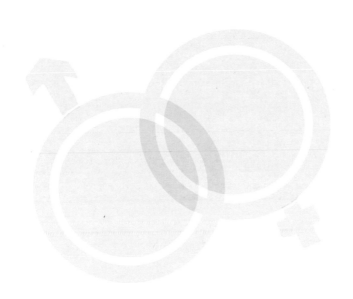

God has no religion.

~ Mahatma Gandhi

A list of the diverse gods that men at one time or another have worshiped would make quite a directory of the changing skies. The supreme deities ran into the hundreds, the minor deities into the thousands . . . Every people in every epoch reinterpreted God after its own fashion, and has been willing to die, or at least to kill, in defense of that passing conception.

~ Will Durant

GOTT MIT UNS

This is the belt buckle Nazi soldiers wore on their uniforms during the Second World War. The buckle reads "God is With Us."

From the beginning men used God to justify the unjustifiable.

~ Salman Rushdie

Man is born broken.

He lives by mending.

The grace of God is glue.

~ Eugene O'Neill

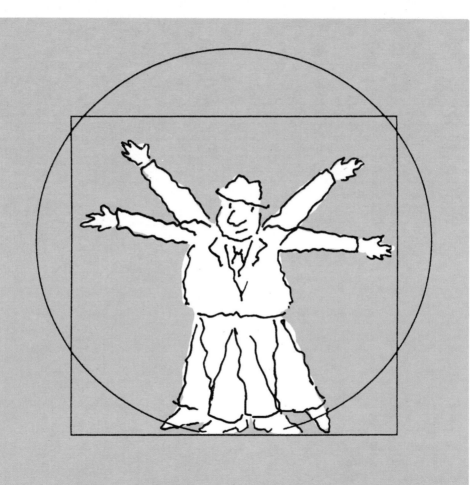

I sometimes think that God, in creating
man, somewhat overestimated his ability.

~ Oscar Wilde

A baby is God's opinion that life should go on.

~ Carl Sandburg

We all ought to understand we're on our own. Believing in Santa Claus doesn't do kids any harm for a few years but it isn't smart for them to continue waiting all their lives for him to come down the chimney with something wonderful. Santa Claus and God are cousins.

~ Andy Rooney

An atheist is a man who has no invisible means of support.

~ John Buchan, Lord Tweedsmuir

Let this be my epitaph: The only proof he needed for the existence of God was music.

~ Kurt Vonnegut

I would only believe in a god
who knew how to dance.

~ Friedrich Nietzsche

Imagination is the voice of daring.
If there is anything godlike about
God, it is that. He dared to imagine
everything.

~ Henry Miller

All Faith is false, all Faith is true:
Truth is the shattered mirror strown
in myriad bits; while each believes
his little bit the whole to own.

~ Sir Richard Francis Burton

BIOGRAPHICAL NOTES

Ansel Adams, 1902–1984
American photographer and environmentalist.

Maya Angelou, 1928–2014
American poet, memoirist, songwriter, playwright, director, producer, civil rights advocate.

Susan B. Anthony, 1820–1906
American social reformer, feminist activist, abolitionist, suffragette.

Julian Barnes, 1946–
English novelist, essayist, winner of the Man Booker Prize.

Charles Baudelaire, 1821–1867
French poet, essayist, art critic, translator.

Tycho Brahe, 1546–1601
Danish nobleman, astronomer, astrologer, alchemist.

Lenny Bruce, 1925–1966
American comedian, social critic, satirist, screenwriter.

John Buchan, Lord Tweedsmuir, 1875–1940
Scottish novelist, historian, and Unionist politician, Govenor General of Canada.

Sir Richard Francis Burton, 1821–1890
English explorer, geographer, writer, cartographer, ethnologist, linguist, poet, diplomat.

George Washington Carver, 1860s–1943
African American, born into slavery, he became a botanist, researcher, inventor, educator, agricultural conservation advocate.

Leonard Cohen, 1934–2016
Canadian singer, songwriter, poet, novelist.

e.e. cummings, 1894–1962
American poet, painter, essayist, author, playwright.

Charles de Montesquieu, 1689–1755
French lawyer, political philosopher, author.

Emily Dickinson, 1830–1886
American poet, almost all of whose 1,800 poems were discovered and published after her death.

Annie Dillard, 1945–
American author, memoirist, poet, educator, essayist, Pulitzer Prize winner.

Frederick Douglass, 1818–1895
African American social reformer, born a slave he escaped to become an abolitionist, orator, writer, and statesman.

Will Durant, 1885–1981
American writer, educator, historian, philosopher, Pulitzer Prize winner.

Thomas Edison, 1847–1931
American inventor of electric lightbulb and phonograph, holder of over 1,000 patents.

Albert Einstein, 1879–1955
German-born theoretical physicist, developer of the theory of relativity, Nobel Prize winner.

Ralph Waldo Emerson, 1803–1882
American poet, essayist, lecturer, leader of the Transcendentalist movement.

Anne Frank, 1929–1945
German-born teen diarist, writer, victim of the Holocaust.

Galileo Galilei, 1564–1642
Italian astronomer, physicist, mathematician, engineer, philosopher.

Mahatma Gandhi, 1869–1948
Indian leader of independence movement, spiritual leader, political activist, proponent of nonviolent civil disobedience.

Jane Goodall, 1934–
English ethologist, primatologist, anthropologist, animal rights activist.

Aldous Huxley, 1894–1963
English novelist, essayist, social satirist, screenwriter, philosopher.

Helen Keller, 1880–1968
American blind and deaf author, political activist, humanitarian, cofounder of the ACLU.

Timothy Leary, 1920–1996
American psychologist and writer, LSD researcher and advocate.

John Lennon, 1940–1980
English singer, songwriter, cofounder of the Beatles, peace activist.

H. L. Mencken, 1880–1956
American journalist, satirist, literary critic.

Donald Miller, 1971–
American author, public speaker, blogger, focusing on Christian spirituality.

Henry Miller, 1891–1980
American author and essayist who created the genre of fictionalized autobiography.

Mother Teresa, 1910–1997
Macedonian Albanian Roman Catholic nun, missionary, humanitarian, Nobel Peace Prize winner, beatified in 2003 by Pope John Paul II.

Friedrich Nietzsche, 1844-1900
German philosopher, cultural critic, poet, philologist, scholar.

Eugene O'Neill, 1888–1953
American playwright, Nobel laureate in Literature.

Pope Francis, 1936–
Argentinean current Pope of the Roman Catholic Church, first Jesuit pope, first from the Americas.

Rainer Maria Rilke, 1875–1926
Bohemian-Austrian poet and novelist.

Andy Rooney, 1919–2011
American radio and television writer, producer, TV commentator.

Salman Rushdie, 1947–
British Kashmiri novelist, essayist, and educator. Knighted in 2007, awarded the PEN/Pinter Prize in 2014.

Rumi, 1207–1273
Persian poet, Islamic scholar, theologian, Sufi mystic.

Mark Sameth, 1954–
American rabbi, author, songwriter.

Carl Sandburg, 1878-1967
American poet, writer, biographer, and editor. Winner of three Pulitzer Prizes.

Kurt Vonnegut, 1922–2007
American novelist, satirist, short-story writer, essayist, playwright.

Alan Watts, 1915–1973
English philosopher, writer, educator,
speaker, popularizer of Eastern philosophy.

Oscar Wilde, 1854–1900
Anglo Irish playwright, novelist, essayist,
poet.

Elie Wiesel, 1928–2016
Romanian-born American writer, professor,
political activist, Nobel Laureate, Holocaust
survivor.

Virginia Woolf, 1882–1941
English novelist, essayist, journalist, feminist.

Frank Lloyd Wright, 1867–1959
American modern architect, designer,
writer, educator, leader of Prairie School
architectural movement.

Malala Yousafzai, 1997–
Pakistani activist for female education,
blogger, youngest-ever Nobel Prize
laureate.

CREDITS

The
End

DATE DUE			